Please Wonderful Mommy

by Anne de Graaf

Illustrated by Evelyn Rivet
© Copyright Scandinavia Publishing House 1992
Published by Scandinavia Publishing House
Nørregade 32, DK-1165, Copenhagen K
Denmark
Text: © Copyright Anne de Graaf 1990
Artwork: © Copyright Evelyn Rivet 1992
Printed in Italy 1996

Published in the United States of America by
Abingdon Press
201 Eighth Avenue South
Nashville, Tennessee 37203

First Abingdon Press Edition 1996
ISBN 0-687-07099-6

TINY TRIUMPHS
PLEASE WONDERFUL MOMMY

By Anne de Graaf
Illustrated by Evelyn Rivet

Dedicated to Erik

Abingdon Press

Daniel was a naughty boy, but not really.
Julia was a naughty girl, but not really.
Mommy was tired of calling them naughty,
really, really.

The two children were naughty because
they didn't like saying please and thank
you.
Instead they grunted, or they didn't
listen.

Every day, before work and after,
Mommy told them,
"Say thank you, say please."
Every time she said it frowns
came and chased the smiles away.
That's when Mommy asked God
for more patience.

This happened at dinner
when Julia pointed at the potatoes.
"Gimme more."
"Say please," smiled Mommy.
Julia grunted, "Mmf."
Mommy frowned, "Naughty girl."

This happened in the shop when the nice lady gave the children candy.

"Say thank you to the nice lady."

The children grunted, "Mmf."

Mommy smiled at the nice lady.

But inside Mommy frowned.

8

This even happened in Grandpa's hospital room, which was no surprise, really, since the frowns had thrown the smiles out of that place a long, long time ago.

When Grandpa gave Julia and Daniel a coin, he frowned.
Mommy tried to smile. "Say thank you."
Julia and Daniel grunted, "Mmf."
Mommy frowned.

On the way home Mommy said,
"You children are very, very naughty. You never say please or thank you. Why should I have such naughty, naughty children?"

Daniel and Julia thought to themselves,
"Maybe we are naughty, but not really."

One day, when Mommy had to go to work and the weather was nice, Mommy's brother Bernard came to visit.

"Here's a present for you, Daniel," Uncle Bernard said.
"Say thank you," whispered Mommy.
"And here's one for you, Julia."
"Say thank you," mumbled Mommy.
Nobody listened and Mommy took her frown to work that day.

12

At dinner that evening Daniel pointed at the potatoes. "Gimme more."

"Say please," smiled Mommy.

Daniel didn't listen.

"What did you say?" Uncle Bernard asked him.
The potatoes steamed at his end of the table.

"Mmf please," said Daniel.

"Please who?" Uncle Bernard's eyes twinkled.

"Please Mommy," said Julia.

"Please what kind of Mommy?"

Mommy looked up. Julia and Daniel shrugged their shoulders.

"What does he mean?"

Uncle Bernard winked at Mommy.

"Please wonderful Mommy."

"Please . . ."

Julia and Daniel giggled. ". . . wonderful Mommy."

A smile ran around the table and chased the frowns away.

This happened in the shop when the nice lady gave the children candy.

"Say thank you to the nice lady."

"Thank you wonderful, nice lady."

Mommy smiled.

But inside Mommy laughed.

This even happened in Grandpa's hospital room.

When Grandpa gave Julia and Daniel a coin,
he frowned.
"Thank you wonderful Grandpa."
And, for the first time since a long, long time ago…
Grandpa smiled.

That's when the smiles threw the frowns out of
that place for good.

On the way home Mommy cried.
She called them good tears.
"Thank you for making Grandpa smile like that."

"Thank you who?"
grinned the children.
Mommy looked up.
Julia and Daniel winked.

"Thank you wonderful
Julia and Daniel."

Daniel and Julia thought
to themselves,
"Yes, we are wonderful."

Now, every day, before work and after, Mommy tells them,

"Please remember to say thank you, wonderful children."

Every time she says it, smiles come and chase the frowns away.

That's when Mommy thanks God for His patience.

Daniel is a wonderful boy, really.
Julia is a wonderful girl, really.
And wonderful Mommy likes calling them wonderful, really, really.